D1152999

EGMONT
We bring stories to life

First published in Great Britain in 2014 by Egmont UK Limited,
The Yellow Building, 1 Nicholas Road, London W11 4AN.

Writer: Kate Graham
Designer: Jeanette Ryall

ISBN 978 1 4052 7204 9
58672/1
Printed in Italy

This Fairies annual
belongs to
Caelan Trousdale
Write your name here.

Disney Fairies

Fawn

Periwinkle

Iridessa

Silvermist

Welcome to Pixie Hollow

Come and explore Pixie Hollow, where Tinker Bell and her fairy friends live. It's a magical place!

Pixie Dust Tree

This huge tree stands in the middle of Pixie Hollow. Deep inside is the Pixie Dust Depot. Ever-so-special pixie dust is kept here, ready to be sprinkled over fairies so they can fly.

1

Queen Clarion watches over the whole of Pixie Hollow from her home. Colour the letters showing where she lives.

Pixie Dust Tree

Spring Valley

Lovely and colourful, Spring Valley is full of young plants bursting into life. Rosetta and other Garden Fairies look after them.

Summer Glade

With the sun always shining, this is a perfect place for the fairies to play. Light Fairy Iridessa lives here in Sunflower Meadow.

Autumn Forest

This forest glows red and orange from the leaves on the trees. The fairies work to keep them these beautiful shades, ready to take to the mainland.

Winter Woods

It is always f-f-f-freezing here! Only Winter Fairies, like Periwinkle, can live in such a cold place without their wings getting damaged.

Answer on page 66.

Hello Tinker Bell

Pixie up-do

Same wings as her sister, Periwinkle

Cute, fairy-green leaf dress

Fairy Facts

Nickname: Tink

Talent: Tinker Fairy

Work: Fixing and inventing things

Loves: Finding bits and bobs and having adventures

Personality: Curious, creative, loyal and full of fun!

Lives in: A tea kettle in Tinker's Nook

Best friends: Terence, a dust-keeper sparrow man, Cheese, a helpful mouse and Blaze, a firefly

Adorable pompoms

Answer on page 66.

Give this fairy-tastic picture of Miss Bell some colour.

Top Tinker Fairy

1

This belongs to Tink. What is it?

Tinkering Trail

Tink is off to meet Periwinkle. Can you help her find the way and collect all the little objects as she goes? She can tinker with them later!

Start

1

Tick the circle when you find this teapot.

Answers on page 66.

2
Tinker Bell and
Periwinkle are cousins.
True
False
Finish
3
How many objects
can Tink collect?
8

A Gift to Fix

Tomorrow is the anniversary of Fawn's arrival, and Tinker Bell wants to make her a special present.
Hmm ... Let's see what I could use ...
SWISH
CLINK

Ooh, this would make a good ...

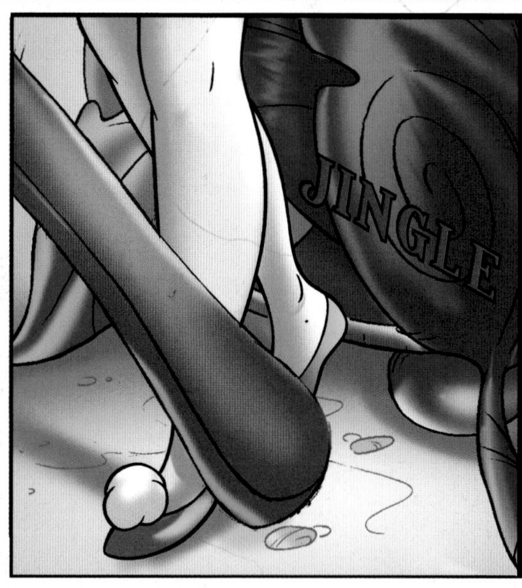
JINGLE

Huh? What just jingled?!

Curiosity gets the better of Tink and ...
Wow!

She doesn't know who left the wonderful object, but Tink knows exactly what to do with it!

The inventive Tinker Fairy gets straight to work!

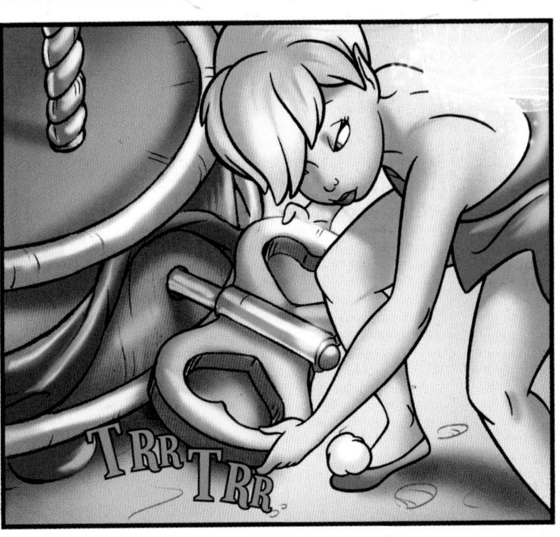

JINGLE TING DING
There! Done!

But suddenly ...
Oh, no!
?!

Terence! Clank, Bobble? What's wrong?
That **musical** thing ...
We **hid** it!

Oh! I saw it and I thought I'd give it to Fawn!
Actually ... it was for **you!**

We wanted to fix it up and give it to you!
I found it on the beach!
Oh!

Sigh! Our surprise is ruined!
No, it isn't!

In fact, you gave me an even **bigger** present!

Not only did you give me a flitterific gift, but you gave me the chance to **repair** it, too!
Gasp! That's right!
Yes, everyone knows how much Tink loves fixing things!

But now I have a surprise for you guys ...
Really?!
Gulp!

I don't have a present for Fawn anymore, so you'll all need to help me make her one!
Huh? **Sure!**
Yes, ma'am! Ha, ha!

THE END

Introducing ...

DISNEY

TINKER BELL AND THE PIRATE FAIRY

Story of the Movie

Zarina is an inquisitive dust-keeper fairy who secretly experiments with making pixie dust. She runs away from Pixie Hollow when she loses her dust-keeping duties because she can't be trusted.

Tinker Bell and her fairy friends realise that *Zarina* has stolen the Blue Pixie Dust that makes the golden pixie dust fairies need to fly, and joined the pirates of Never Land. When they try to retrieve the Blue Dust, *Zarina* blasts them with a pixie dust concoction. This switches all their talents around - and their outfits, too!

Zarina has grown a huge tree at Never Land's Skull Rock. From there, she wants to make enough pixie dust to make the pirates' ship fly!

Can the Pixie Hollow fairies stop *Zarina* and claim back the precious Blue Pixie Dust?

Zarina

Zarina is a lively and curious fairy. But her sense of adventure gets her into real trouble!

Cabin boy *James* is kind to Zarina at first. She thinks he's her best friend, but he's really the cunning captain of the pirates!

Fairy Gary gets so angry with Zarina for tampering with the pixie dust, that he bans her from being a dust-keeper.

Add some magical colour to the pirate ship.

This is the motley crew of *Never Land pirates* that Tink and friends have to brave in their quest to save the Blue Pixie Dust.

Rosetta is the first living thing cute *Baby Crocodile* sees on hatching from his egg. He thinks Rosetta is his mother!

Disney Tinker Bell and the Pirate Fairy

Adventure Time

Fly away with the fairies and help them solve these tricky treasers!

Croc Check

Can you spot four differences between these two pictures of Rosetta and her little croc friend?

a

b

Tongue Twister

Tink keeps getting her words all in a muddle. Can you say this sentence really fast, three times in a row?

Quick, pick up the pixie dust!

Quick, pick up the pixie dust!

Quick, pick up the pixie dust!

Answers on page 66.

Jolly James

Which of the items below should James be holding in his right hand to complete his best pirate outfit?

Light Up!

Can you put the lantern back together again by re-arranging the picture pieces? It's easy to see which piece goes at the top!

Pick a Picture

Look carefully at the pictures below. See if you can spot the odd one out in each row. Circle it with a pencil.

Disney
Tinker Bell
and the
Pirate Fairy
Cut along here

Disney
Tinker Bell
AND THE
PIRATE FAIRY
Cut along here.

Whose Shadow?

See if you can work out which shadow belongs to which character. Who is left without a shadow?

Tinker Bell

a

b

Zarina

c

d

Port

James

Baby Croc

All Mixed Up

Use these pictures to help you read this story about Zarina's mischief.

Tinker Bell | Zarina | Pirates | Blue Pixie Dust

 and her fairy friends could not believe what had happened.  had just blasted them with some of her own pixie dust and switched their talents.  had become a water talent fairy. Vidia's new talent was tinkering and she wasn't happy! Rosetta loved the pink dress that she wore as a garden fairy, but now she had become an animal fairy, with a dress to match! "Look at my outfit," she groaned.

None of the fairies had escaped the powerful trick that  had played. Iridessa's light talent had changed to a garden talent. Silvermist was now a fast-flying fairy, and Fawn had become a light fairy!

"We're all mixed up, that's for sure," declared .

But mixed up talents were not going to stop the fairies rescuing the  that  had stolen and taken to the . Their friendship would help them succeed, even if their new talents and dresses did feel very strange indeed!

THE END

Look at this action-packed scene aboard the pirate ship, then answer the questions about it.

What is Zarina doing?

Singing Fighting

Search carefully for this detail in the picture.

How many lanterns can you spot?

Point to the pirate who is flying! What is his name?

Starboard James

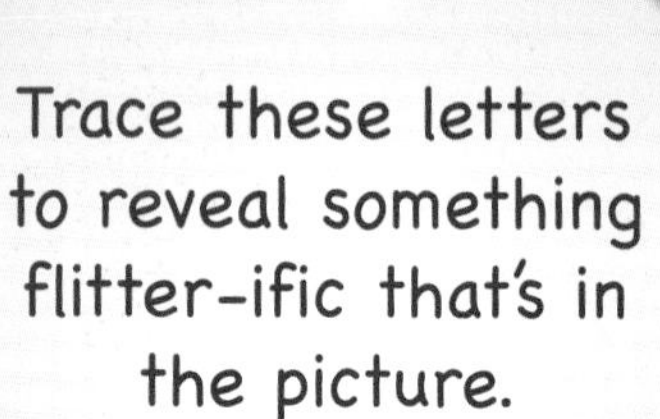

Trace these letters to reveal something flitter-ific that's in the picture.

Wings

Answers on page 66.

Disney
Tinker Bell and the Pirate Fairy
Bring this Pirate Fairy-tastic scene to life by colouring Tinker Bell and Zarina!

Hello Rosetta

Girly, long locks

Flitter-ific wings

Pink, rose petal fashion

Pretty pumps

Fairy Facts

Nickname: Ro
Talent: Garden Fairy
Work: Caring for flowers & plants
Loves: Looking after flowers and plants
Personality: Sweet, funny, sharing and caring
Lives in: Rose-blossom chalet in Buttercup Canyon
Best friends: She loves her potted plants (and even tells them bedtime stories!)

Answer on page 66.

A Colourful Surprise

Rosetta's eyes are barely open, when something attracts her attention.
Wow! Check out the colours on that baby bird!

If only every creature looked that good ...
As Rosetta gets ready for the day ahead, she can't stop thinking how stylish the robin redbreast looks.

And suddenly, Rosetta has an idea! After gathering everything she'll need, she flies off to begin her plan.

Let's go find Rosetta now!
It's the middle of the afternoon by the time Tink and Fawn realize they haven't seen their friend all day.

But on their way to Rosetta's garden, the fairies run into a strange-looking squirrel ...
Look at his chest! Something funny is going on here!

Finally Tink and Fawn track down their fairy friend – plus a queue of animals waiting to have their chests painted!
Hi, girls! Hold still, Buttercup, I'm almost done!

Tink and Fawn can't believe their eyes, so Rosetta explains all about the robin redbreast.
I wanted every creature to look just as special!

Fawn laughs, and tells Rosetta that those are the robin's NATURAL colours.

She and Tink explain that all their forest friends are created differently, just as all fairies have a different talent - and that's exactly how things should be.
You two are right. Differences are what make us special!
Exactly! Now, let's clean up all these "red-bellies". Ha ha!
THE END

Party Puzzle

Rosetta is going to a party and she wants to wear her favourite dress. Use the clues below to help her pick it out.

Now put a tick next to the right dress!

Answer on page 66.

Fancy Dress

The fairies are watching Rosetta show off her dressing-up costume. What fun! But can you spot five differences in the bottom picture?

Colour a flower each time you find a difference.

Answers on page 66.

Hello Fawn

Fairy Facts

Nickname: She's just Fawn to everyone!
Talent: Animal Fairy
Work: Helps animals in need
Loves: Loves playing tricks on her friends
Personality: Caring, lively, mischievous, and brave
Lives in: A giant pine cone in Pine Forest
Best friends: Tinker Bell and Rosetta

1
Can you spot
a ladybird
somewhere on
the page?
Brighten up Fawn
and colour her in
using the colours
shown below.
brown
orange
yellow
black
green
Ace Animal Fairy

Forest Magic

There's always heaps to do deep in the forest. Can you help Fawn solve these mini teasers?

Picnic Time

Look at this picnic scene, then cover it with a piece of paper and see how many questions you can answer.

a) What two colours is the cake?

b) Who is wearing a pink dress?

c) What colour is Fawn's hairband?

Tweet, Tweet!

Can you put these sweet birds in order of size, starting with the biggest?

a b c d

Biggest ... Smallest

Berry Clever

Can you match these berries into pairs? Circle the berry that doesn't have a match.

a b c d e

Count

Count the pine cones hiding on these pages.

Flower Blooms

How many of each colour flower has been picked by the fairies?

Answers on page 66.

Flying Fun!

One spring day, Tink is feeling completely uninspired. All the other fairies are working on their talents, but she has no idea what to make!

Tink is deep in thought, when suddenly she hears a voice ...
Spread your wings, little friend!

It sounds like Fawn's voice, coming from high above the ground!
C'mon, move those feathers!

Sounds like there could be trouble ... Tink decides to follow Fawn's voice to investigate further!
FRRRR

Near the top of the tree, Tink finds Fawn trying to teach a baby bird to fly!

But things don't seem to be going very well ...

When Fawn abandons her wings and tries to pull the bird out of his nest, Tink decides that it's time to lend a hand!

Coming closer, she asks Fawn what the problem is and offers to help.

But Tink's best efforts don't seem to be helping either ...

... even when she orders him to fly!

Finally, Fawn thinks she's come up with a plan.

Since the bird is so little, Fawn thinks that perhaps he doesn't realize how fun flying can be!

But how to convince him?

Tink flies off to get to work ...

A couple of wing-beats later, Tink returns with an amazing flying machine!

Not wanting to miss the fun, it isn't long before the baby bird is soaring through the air with Tink and Fawn!

Hello Periwinkle

Fairy Facts

Nickname: Peri
Talent: Frost Fairy
Work: Frosting the leaves of Winter Woods
Loves: Making frost swirls and sledging down frozen waterfalls!
Personality: Curious and fun-loving, just like Tink!
Lives in: The Winter Woods, where it's cold all year round
Best friends: Spike and Gliss

Fabulous Frost Fairy

1

How many snowflakes can you count?

Use your best pens to make Peri shimmer with colour.

Winter Wonderland
Have fun with Periwinkle in the Winter Woods solving these frosty puzzles!
Pattern Match
a
b
c
d
e
Only one set of these pretty wings is exactly the same as Tinker Bell and Periwinkle's. Can you find it?

Busy Owls

The snowy owls are delivering baskets filled with sparkling snowflakes. Help them by matching each piece below to the correct space in the big picture.

Answers on page 66.

Neat and nice style

Special sunflower seed

Buttercup and sunflower petals rule!

Sweet sandals

Fairy Facts

Nickname: Dess

Talent: Light Fairy

Work: Creates light so plants can grow

Loves: Helping the Water Fairies make rainbows

Personality: Happy, warm and sensible

Lives in: A big, yellow sunflower

Best friends: Great pals with the fireflies who she lights up at night

Answer on page 66.

Join the dots to complete the picture. Then colour in Iridessa so she lights up the page!
1
Iridessa's dress is pink.
True
False
Lovely Light Fairy

Panic Over Petals

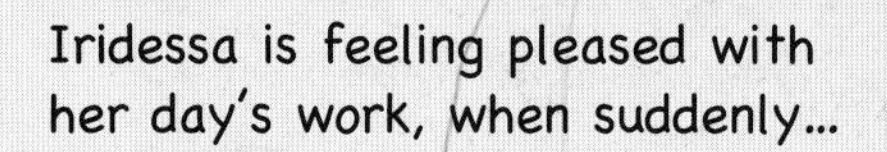

CONCEPT AND SCRIPT: TEA ORSI; LAYOUT, CLEANUP: MONICA CATALANO; PENCIL REVISION: SARA STORINO; INKS: SANTA ZANGARI; COLOR: STUDIO KAWAII

So Silvermist adds more dew, but...

Gulp! Maybe I overdid it!

The fairies remove the beads of dew, hoping this will perk the flower back up – but nothing changes.
What now? How am I going to tell Ro?

Silvermist reassures Iridessa that everyone makes mistakes sometimes.

Except me, usually ... sigh. But you're right, I'll tell her everything now!

The fairies call Rosetta over, and Iridessa prepares to break the bad news.

Right. Um, actually ...
Sorry, sugarplum! Give me just one second.

To Iridessa's dismay, Rosetta heads straight for the wilted violet. But she doesn't SEEM angry...

You're the most graceful violet in all Pixie Hollow. That's it, look at those petals!

Suddenly the violet is prettier than ever, and only Rosetta knows why. She explains that this particular violet is so shy that she's always shrinking.
But with a few compliments she perks right up!

So, what was it you wanted to tell me?
Oh, nothing ...
Iridessa had learned that even those with great talents can make small mistakes, but she was definitely grateful for this surprise ending!
THE END

Help Iridessa find a route through the maze to reach the fireflies in the middle. The buckets of sunlight will light her way!

START

FINISH

1

Count the leaf buckets of sunlight along the path Iridessa takes.

Answers on page 66.

Fairy Finds

Iridessa and Fawn have been collecting things. Their collections are almost exactly the same, except for one item.

1

Can you circle the extra item that each fairy has found?

Answers on page 66.

Hello Silvermist

Fairy Facts

Nickname: Sil

Talent: Water Fairy

Work: Sprinkling plants with water, carrying water droplets to creatures

Loves: Sending secret messages to her friends in a bubble!

Personality: Kind, calm and sympathetic to her friends

Lives in: Next to Lilypad Pond, with a waterfall nearby

Best friends: She just loves to get along with everyone!

Use the spots to help you colour Silvermist.

1

Follow the trail to see where it leads.

Wonderful Water Fairy

Answer on page 66.

Silvermist's Show

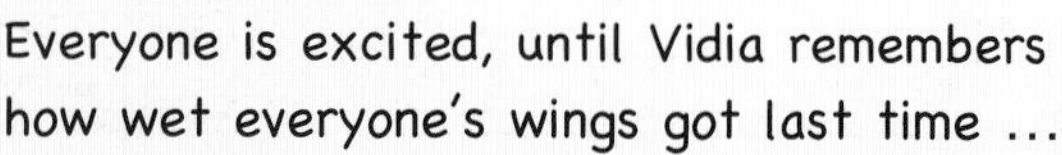

Tink collects the right leaves for the umbrellas and heads to her workshop.
I'm going to decorate them with each person's favourite things!
Collecting supplies along the way.

And so Tink begins her search.

Scented rose petals for Rosetta! I love them, even if they make me sneeze!

And feathers for Vidia ...

... acorns for Fawn ...

... although a hungry squirrel
isn't too happy about that!

Don't worry,
I'm only taking
the caps!

And finally, some sparkly
gems for Iridessa.
Time to get
to work!

Later that night, Tink presents her friends with their finished umbrellas.
Wow, they're beautiful!

Then Iridessa points out a tiny problem ...
But where's your leaf umbrella, Tink?

Tink has been so busy, she completely forgot to make herself an umbrella! She thinks she'll just have to get a little wet, but it's Vidia's turn to come up with a plan.

Thank you! You girls are true friends!
The fairies share their umbrellas, so they can all stay dry together and enjoy Silvermist's fountains.
THE END

Answers

Page 8 Welcome to Pixie Hollow

1) Queen Clarion lives in the Pixie Dust Tree.

Page 10 Hello Tinker Bell

1) It is Tinker Bell's hammer.

Page 12 Tinkering Trail

1) The teapot is next to the big daisy.
2) False. They are sisters.
3) There are 8 objects to collect.

Page 20 Adventure Time

Croc Check:

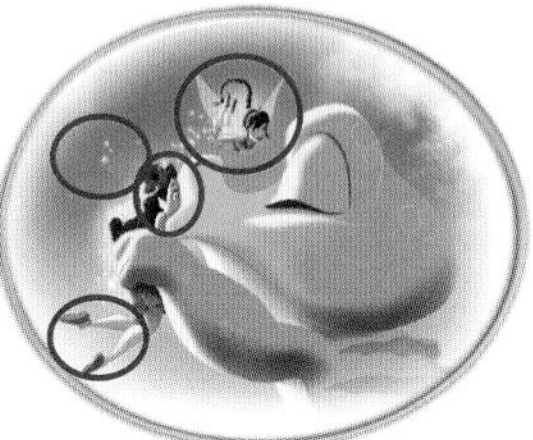

Jolly James: c.

Light Up!: d, c, a, b.

Page 22 Pick a Picture

1) d, 2) c, 3) b, 4) There are 4 keys.

Page 25 Whose Shadow?

a – Baby Croc, b – Tinker Bell, c – Zarina, d – James. Port doesn't have a shadow.

Page 28 Fairy Action

1) Fighting. 2) It's the buckle on James' belt. 3) There are 6 lanterns. 4) Starboard. 5) Wings.

Page 32 Hello Rosetta

1) The pink rose.

Page 38 Party Puzzle

Dress number 5.

Page 39 Fancy Dress

Page 40 Hello Fawn

1) The ladybird is in the bottom right hand corner of the page, next to the squirrel.

Page 42 Forest Magic

Picnic Time: 1) Red and white. 2) Rosetta. 3) Green.

Tweet, Tweet!: a, c, d, b.

Berry Clever: b and e, c and d. Fruit a doesn't have a match.

Fairy Blooms: white – 4, pink – 2, purple – 3, yellow – 5.

Count: 3 pine cones.

Page 48 Hello, Periwinkle

1) There are 7 snowflakes, including the one next to the question.

Page 50 Winter Wonderland

Pattern Match: c.

Busy Owls: 1 – d, 2 – a, 3 – g, 4 – b, 5 – f, 6 – e, 7 – h, 8 – c.

Page 52 Hello, Iridessa

1) False, it's yellow.

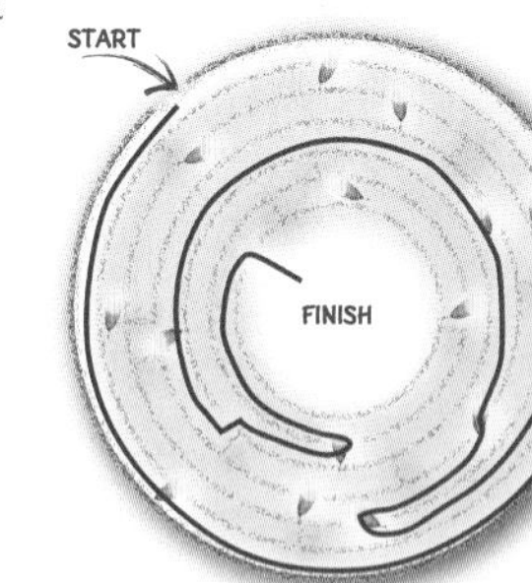

Page 58 Maze Search

1. 7.

Page 59 Fairy Finds

Iridessa has found a shell mobile. Fawn has found a leaf mirror.

Page 60 Hello, Silvermist

1) The trail leads to the yellow butterfly.

Disney
FAIRIES
Cut along here

Disney
Fairies
Cut along here.